Heartsongs
&
Journey
Through
Heartsongs

Heartsongs
&
Journey
Through
Heartsongs

Written and Illustrated by
Mattie J. T. Stepanek
Poet and Peacemaker

Thorndike Press • Waterville, Maine

Published in 2002 by arrangement with Hyperion,
an imprint of Buena Vista Books, Inc.

Thorndike Press Large Print Americana Series.

The tree indicium is a trademark of Thorndike Press.

The text of this Large Print edition is unabridged.
Other aspects of the book may vary from the original edition.

Cover illustration by Mattie J. T. Stepanek.

Set in 16 pt. Plantin by Elena Picard.

Printed in the United States on permanent paper.

Library of Congress Cataloging-in-Publication Data

Stepanek, Mattie J. T. (Mattie Joseph Thaddeus.)
    Heartsongs ; and, Journey through heartsongs / written
and illustrated by Mattie J. T. Stepanek.
        p. cm. — (Thorndike Press large print Americana series)
    ISBN 0-7862-4432-1 (lg. print : hc : alk. paper)
    1. Muscular dystrophy in children — Patients — Poetry.
2. Large type books. I. Title: Heartsongs ; and, Journey
through heartsongs. II. Stepanek, Mattie J. T. (Mattie
Joseph Thaddeus). Journey through heartsongs.
III. Title: Journey through heartsongs. IV. Title. V. Series.
PS3619.T4765 H43 2002
    813'.54—dc21   2002067599

Contents

Heartsongs 13

Journey Through Heartsongs 57

Heartsongs

Contents

Senses   13

Seasons   25

Celebrations   37

Dedication

This book is dedicated to those who believe in celebrating the gifts of life every day, especially my mom, all of my kin, and the entire staff of the Pediatric Intensive Care Unit at Children's National Medical Center. Always remember to play after every storm!

Making Real Sense of the Senses

Our eyes are for looking at things,
But they are also for crying
When we are very happy or very sad.
Our ears are for listening,
But so are our hearts.
Our noses are for smelling food,
But also the wind and the grass and
If we try very hard, butterflies.
Our hands are for feeling,
But also for hugging and touching so
    gently.
Our mouths and tongues are for
    tasting,
But also for saying words, like
"I love you," and
"Thank you, God, for all of these
things."

The Gift of Color

Thank You
For all the colors of the rainbow.
Thank You
For sharing these colors
With all of the fish
And all of the birds
And all of the flowers
That You have given us.
And thank You
For the colors of the
Heaven-in-the-earth
And of the
Heaven-in-the-sky,
And for sharing these colors
In the people of the world.
You give us color
As a gift, God,
And I thank You

For all of these
Beautiful colors and
Beautiful things and
Beautiful people.
What special gifts
You have given to us!

The Smell of a Noise

Shhhh . . .
I smell something.
It smells like a noise.
Like a turtle noise.
Yes, that's what it is.
It is a turtle noise,
And it is wonderful,
Because turtles
Live inside of seashells.
Would you like to
Live in a seashell?
It would smell like
A turtle noise,
But I think
It would be wonderful!

Angel-Wings

This morning,
I smelled something very good.
Perhaps,
It was a rainbow.
Or maybe,
It was a dinosaur smile.
Or even,
A seashell.
I am not sure
What I smelled.
And I am not sure
What rainbows
Or dinosaur smiles
Or seashells
Smell like.
But I'm sure they smell wonderful.
Wonderful and special
Like the smell of

Angel-Wings.
But also,
I'm sure they smell
A little sad,
Because we can't really smell
A rainbow,
Or a dinosaur smile,
Or a seashell,
Or especially,
We can't really smell
The wonderful smell
Of Angel-Wings.

Very Special Candy

One day,
I will make a bag of
Very Special Candy.
The candy will come in
All different colors,
Colors like you see in
Good Ordinary Candy.
But . . .
The flavors will be
So different and
So special and
So wonderful.
There will be little
Blue candies
That taste like sky.
And the little
Green and brown candies
Will taste like grass and trees.

The orange ones
Will taste like butterfly,
The yellow ones
Like flowers and sunshine,
And the white ones
Like clouds in Heaven.
And then,
I will make a very, very
Special piece of candy,
That is all different colors
And that glows like a halo.
And that will be the one
That tastes like
Rainbow and Angels.

When My Feet Itch

When my feet itch,
Maybe I'll think about
Riding on a dinosaur
With my mom —
And then,
I won't remember that my feet itch.
When my feet itch,
Maybe I'll think about
Spending the night at the
North Pole with Santa Claus —
And then,
It will be too cold for my feet to itch.
When my feet itch,
Maybe I'll think about
Playing with Nick and Ben
Because they're some of the
Best friends a kid could ever have —
And then,

I won't care if my feet itch or not.
Or maybe, when my feet itch,
I'll think about angels —
Because they don't make
You itch when you touch them.

Seasons

Leaf for a Day

Today,
I think I will be a tree.
Or perhaps,
A leaf on a branch on the tree.
I will feel
The gentle breeze,
And then I will
'Plip' off of my branch and my tree
And float in the wind.
I will go
Back and forth in the breeze
All the way down to the ground.
And after I rest
And say 'hello'
To the grass and dirt and bugs,
I will call to the wind,
'Come and take me
To visit my other leaf-friends

On all of the other trees, please.'
And the gentle breeze
Will come
And pick me up
So that I can jump and dance
With all of the other
Tree-stars and tree-flowers
That God gave the world.
What a special idea
To be, today.

On the Mountain of Tree-Stars

Summer is almost over.
Soon, it will be September.
And then, it will be fall.
And when it is fall,
We can play with all
The tree-stars that fall
To us from up high.
And when the tree-stars fall
From the sky,
We can build a leaf-mountain.
First, when all
The leaves fall
From the sky,
We put them all
Together into a mountain-pile
Way up high.
Then, we get a string and tie
Them all
Together so that when

The wind blows they won't fly
Away from the mountain-pile.
And last, we climb
Up the leaf-mountain,
And we stand up so high
Next to the sky,
And then — sliiiiiiide —
We slide
Aaaaaaaaalll
The way to the bottom of the
    mountain-leaf pile.
So when the fall
Comes it will get chilly,
And things will start to fall
Like the season.
But they don't fall
With a boom!
Only they fall
Like a floating leaf, or
Like a little boy on
The Mountain of Tree-Stars.

Winter Luck

Snowflakes . . .
They come down so slow,
And sometimes so fast,
Looking like pretty stars
Falling down, down, down
To the ground.
Little stars with little holes,
Bigger stars with bigger holes,
They are all cuddly snowflake stars.
Snowflakes of the tiny snows,
Snowstars of the bigger snows,
I will catch you on my hand
Or on my tongue
And make a wish . . .
I will make a wish on
My falling snowstar,
And then have good luck
All day, all night, all Ever.

Important Things

When I grow up,
I think maybe
I will be a snowman,
Because when it
Snows outside,
I'll already be cold
And like it.
And children will
Play with me,
And laugh
And sing
And dance
All around me.
And those are important
Things to have happen
When you grow up.

Indian Winter

Hey!
It's cold out here today!
This is May,
And it's supposed to be
Spring
Turning into
Summer,
So I can have my birthday.
But I need my jacket,
And my hat.
Oh, bother!
I wonder —
Who played with the seasons
Last night
While we were all sleeping?

The Eye of the Beholder

Dandelions are NOT weeds!
See?
They have beautiful
Yellow flowers on them.
They have lovely
Green stems.
Mommy puts them
In a jar of water
In the kitchen —
They are flowers!
See?
They are round.
They are round and yellow.
Oh, mommy,
Please tell him
He's making a big mistake!
Poor little dandelions . . .
He's pulling them all up

And calling them "weeds."
Oh, this is
So horrible, so sad!
What would God say if
He saw you sending all of these
Poor, little, round, yellow
Dandelion-flowers
Back to the Lord?

Summer 'Rememberies'

After everyone has
A smoky cookout at Chip's house,
And the grown-ups make
Music on their guitars for singing
   and dancing,
And the children take
Off their shoes and run
Around the backyard catching
Lightning bugs in the dark —
Then, it is a very good time to be
Happy.
And that 'then' is
A very good time and
A very good feeling to remember
Ever-after.

The Importance of Windows

Windows are very good things to have.
They let you look out,
And see all the different things.
And they let you look in,
To see all the other different things.
And do you know what is the most
Special window of all?
The window in your heart,
That's between the Heaven-in-the-
   earth,
And the Heaven-in-the-sky.

Circle of Happiness

I am a little kid
For you to love.
I am a little kid
For you to hug and kiss.
I am a little kid
For you to say,
"You are so special,
Yes you are" to.
I am a little kid
For all of those things
And more.
And when you
Feel and say and do
All of those things,
I will be a little kid
Who will love you.
I will be a little kid
Who will hug and kiss you.

I will be a little kid
Who will say to you,
"You are so special, too,
Yes you are."
I will be a little kid
Who will do all of those things
And more.
And that is what
Happiness
Is all about.

On Being Thankful

Dear God,
I was going to thank You tonight
For a beautiful sunrise,
That was pink behind the fog down
   the hill,
And for a wonderful rainbow,
That I ran under pointing to
All my favorite colors,
And for such a great sunset,
That sparkled orange across the water.
I was going to thank You tonight
For all of these special gifts,
Except that none of them happened.
But do You know what?
I still love You, God,
And I have lots of other things
That I can thank You for tonight,
Even if you didn't give those

Very special gifts to me today.
It's okay, God,
Because I'll look for them all again,
When my tomorrow comes.
Amen.

Pinch of Peace

Dear God,
Tonight my prayers are for the world.
We have to stop this fighting.
We have to stop the wars.
People need to lay down their
    weapons,
And find peace in their hearts.
People need to stop arguing and
    hating.
People need to notice the good things.
People need to remember You, God.
Maybe You could come and
Shoot a little bow-and-arrow pinch
Into all the angry peoples' hearts,
    God.
Then they would feel You again.
And then they would realize what
They are doing and how horrible the

Killing and hating and fighting is,
And they might even begin to pray.
Then, they could reach in, and
Pull the little bow-and-arrow pinch
Out of their hearts and feel good
And be loving and living people again.
And then,
The world would be at peace, and
The children would be safe, and
The people would be happy, and
We could all say "thank You"
    together.
Amen.

Heartsong

I have a song, deep in my heart,
And only I can hear it.
If I close my eyes and sit very still
It is so easy to listen to my song.
When my eyes are open and
I am so busy and moving and
    busy,
If I take time and listen very hard,
I can still hear my Heartsong.
It makes me feel happy.
Happier than ever.
Happier than everywhere
And everything and everyone
In the whole wide world.
Happy like thinking about
Going to Heaven when I die.
My Heartsong sounds like this —

46

I love you! I love you!
How happy you can be!
How happy you can make
This whole world be!
And sometimes it's other
Tunes and words, too,
But it always sings the
Same special feeling to me.
It makes me think of
Jamie, and Katie and Stevie,
And other wonderful things.
This is *my* special song.
But do you know what?
All people have a special song
Inside their hearts!
Everyone in the whole wide world
Has a special Heartsong.
If you believe in magical, musical
    hearts,
And if you believe you *can* be happy,
Then you, too, will hear *your* song.

The Daily Gift

You know what?
Tomorrow is a new day.
And today is a new day.
Actually,
Every day is a new day.
Thank You, God,
For all of these
Special and new days.

About the Author

I am Mattie J. T. Stepanek.
My body has light skin,
Red blood, blue eyes, and blond hair.
Since I have mitochondrial myopathy,
I even have a trach, a ventilator, and
    oxygen.
Very poetic, I am, and very smart, too.
I am always brainstorming ideas and
    stories.
I am a survivor, but some day,
    I will see
My two brothers and one sister
    in Heaven.
When I grow up, I plan to become
A daddy, a writer, a public speaker,
And most of all, a peacemaker.
Whoever I am, and whatever happens,
I will always love my body and mind,

Even if it has different abilities
Than other peoples' bodies and
    minds.
I will always be happy, because
I will always be me.

Eleven-year-old Matthew Joseph Thaddeus Stepanek, best known as "Mattie," has been writing poetry and short stories since age three. Mattie's poems have been published in a variety of mediums and he has been an

© Jim Hawkins

invited speaker for several seminars, conferences and television shows. In 1999, he was awarded the Melinda Lawrence International Book Award for inspirational written works by the Children's Hospice International. He has appeared on *Oprah*, *The Today Show*, *Good Morning America* and many other programs. In addition to writing, Mattie enjoys reading, collecting rocks and shells, and playing with Legos. He has earned a black belt in martial arts, and in 2001, Mattie served as the Maryland State Goodwill Ambassador for the Muscular Dystrophy Association. In 2002, he will serve as both the National Ambassador and the State Ambassador for the MDA. He lives with his mother, Jeni, in Upper Marlboro, MD, where he is home-schooled.

The publishers wish to acknowledge the assistance and support of the following people in the production of this book: Martha Shaw Whitley, our amazing sister, for organizing and coordinating the people and events which allow Mattie's book to be shared far and wide; Marissa L. Garis, public relations and marketing specialist at Children's National Medical Center for introducing us to Mattie and his mom, Jeni, and giving us the opportunity to publish Mattie's poems; Catherine Morrison, our production director, who tries to keep us all organized; and Jeni Stepanek, Mattie's mom, whose hidden talents as an editor are greatly appreciated.

Peter and Cheryl Barnes
VSP Books
Alexandria, Virginia
June 2001

Journey
Through
Heartsongs

Dedication

This book is dedicated to Katie, Stevie and Jamie, and to all the other angels, saints and blessed ones who guide, guard and protect me, especially Jude Thaddeus, Rita and Andre Bisset.

— Love, Mattie

Dear Friends,

Mattie and his mother, Jeni, are two of the most extraordinary people we have been privileged to meet. As this book shows, Mattie, poet and peacemaker, is a gifted writer with a powerful message for those seeking hope, faith and answers. We thank God for blessing us with the opportunity to publish Mattie's books and to help spread his messages of hope, peace, wisdom and insight to people everywhere.

But we could not have done it alone. We wish to acknowledge the following people for their help and support in producing this book: our mom, Shirley Shaw, for showing up at the office every day and leading the charge with joy and enthusiasm; our dad, Chuck Shaw, for keeping us organized and well fed during this busy time; Martha Shaw Whitley, our amazing sister for all of her hard work; Marissa L. Garis of the Children's National Medical Center in Washington, DC, for introducing us to Mattie and Jeni; our webmaster, David Schaefer, for keeping our website constantly up-to-date; and Catherine Morrison in our office, for keeping the production line going. We also want to thank: Jeff Riggs; George Muriithi; Moshe Koenick; Ron Cofone; Lisa Delnegro; Kim

Turpin Davis; Rep. Fred Upton (R-MI); Ron Landsman, attorney-at-law; Tim O'Brien, attorney-at-law; Sharon Taylor; and the Encouragers Class at First Baptist Church of Alexandria, VA, which planted the seed.

And, most of all, Mattie and Jeni.

Peter and Cheryl Barnes
Publishers

September 2001

Acknowledgments

I would like to thank Dr. Robert Fink, Dr. Christie Corrveaux, Dr. Kim Fenton, and everybody at the Pediatric Intensive Care Unit at Children's National Medical Center in Washington, DC, for believing in my life and my future.

I would like to thank Peter and Cheryl Barnes, Shirley Shaw, Martha Whitley, Marissa Garis, and Maggie and Kate Jerde for believing in my dreams.

I would like to thank the Muscular Dystrophy Association, Jerry Lewis, Children's Hospice International, Harold Schaitberger and the International Association of Fire Fighters, the Harley-

Davidson Owners Group, the D'Anna "MARS" Family, United Airlines and many others for believing in hope towards a cure.

I would like to thank Jimmy Carter, my "humble peacemaker" hero, and Oprah Winfrey, Ed McMahon, Rosie O'Donnell, Martin Doblmeier, Jeanne Myers and Steven Spielberg for believing in and fulfilling the wishes of children.

I would like to thank Sandy, Heather, Jamie-D., Chris, Lyn, Mike, Nick, Ben, Shana, Bubby, Flora, Paul, Don, Lorraine, Clifton, Valerie, Mollie, Katie, Annie, Ron, Devin, Gina, Ann, Casey, Jim, Andi, Leslie, Bert, J.J., Randy, Roger, Holy Rosary and many other kin-family for believing in and supporting the journey through Heartsongs.

And, I would like to thank my mom, Jeni, for believing in all of these things and in the daily celebration of life and spirit. I love you and you love me, forever and always.

— Love
Mattie J. T. Stepanek

Foreword

Mattie Stepanek is my personal friend and one of the most remarkable young people I have ever known. He wants to be a peacemaker; and through his poems and own courageous example, he proves that finding peace within one's self can lead to harmony among families, communities and nations. With wisdom and uncomplicated vision Mattie reminds us how easy it is to forgive others, to find something amazing even in the most trivial things and to celebrate the little gifts of life each day.

Journey Through Heartsongs will inspire readers of all ages with thoughts and images that bring both tears and expanded hearts.

— Jimmy Carter
Former U.S. President

Contents

Beginning the Journey   73

Considering the Journey   97

Coping with the Journey   115

Celebrating the Journey   137

Growing Beyond the Journey   155

Prayer for a Journey

Thank You, God,
Not just for life,
But for our journey through life.
Life is a miracle,
And a journey through life
Is so full of so many more miracles
If we travel with our Heartsongs.
Thank You, God,
For blessing me with the
Gift of Heartsongs,
So that I can enjoy my miracles.

April 1998

About the Author

I am Mattie J. T. Stepanek.
My body has light skin,
Red blood, blue eyes, and blond hair.
Since I have mitochondrial myopathy,
I even have a trach, a ventilator, and
    oxygen.
Very poetic, I am, and very smart, too.
I am always brainstorming ideas and
    stories.
I am a survivor, but some day,
    I will see
My two brothers and one sister
    in Heaven.
When I grow up, I plan to become
A father, a writer, a public speaker,
And most of all, a peacemaker.
Whoever I am, and whatever happens,
I will always love my body and mind,

Even if it has different abilities
Than other peoples' bodies and
   minds.
I will always be happy, because
   I will always be me.

                              May 2001

Heartsong

I have a song, deep in my heart,
And only I can hear it.
If I close my eyes and sit very still
It is so easy to listen to my song.
When my eyes are open and
I am so busy and moving and
   busy,
If I take time and listen very hard,
I can still hear my Heartsong.
It makes me feel happy.
Happier than ever.
Happier than everywhere
And everything and everyone
In the whole wide world.
Happy like thinking about
Going to Heaven when I die.
My Heartsong sounds like this —

I love you! I love you!
How happy you can be!
How happy you can make
This whole world be!
And sometimes it's other
Tunes and words, too,
But it always sings the
Same special feeling to me.
It makes me think of
Jamie, and Katie and Stevie,
And other wonderful things.
This is *my* special song.
But do you know what?
All people have a special song
Inside their hearts!
Everyone in the whole wide world
Has a special Heartsong.
If you believe in magical, musical hearts,
And if you believe you *can* be happy,
Then you, too, will hear *your* song.

March 1996

Crystal Celebration

Sometimes,
Sunrise is like a heavenly crystal ball.
Everyday,
In the little bit of time between night
    and day,
The Angels look at the earth
To see how things have been and
To see how things are going and
To see how things will be.
The sky changes from dark
Into Angel-whites and Angel-golds.
The blackness of trees starts to glow
    with
Pinks and purples and oranges from
    their hearts.
And during each dawn,
All the Angels gather up and have
A celebration in God's honor!

And sometimes,
You can even watch
And join them in the celebrating.
Just look out into the sunrise,
Then jump into your own heart,
Float into the air like in a dream,
And pray with love and praise and
    thank-yous
For your life, for your spirit, for your
sunrise . . .
And for being a part of this heavenly
crystal ball!

December 1996

For Mr. Thompson

The people who like poetry are
   special.
They are the same people who hear
Lullabies and wind chimes
When the birds are noisy together.
They are the ones who see
Star-gifts in every season —
Tree-stars in the fall,
Snow-stars in the winter,
Dandelion-fairy-stars in the spring,
   and
Lightning-bug-stars in the summer.
They are the ones who have
Favorite colors that are wonderful
   gifts
Like sunset or rainbow or treasure.
They are the ones who have a
Song in their heart and

Words in their mind that
Come together and slip out
Into the air or onto paper as a gift
To someone else, or even themselves.
The people who like poetry are
    probably
The ones who really like life,
And who know how to celebrate
Even when things are sad or happy.
We remember that sometimes,
Even if we don't understand why,
That the rain falls for a reason.
We remember how important it is
To play after a storm, just because
We need to keep playing and living.
And, we are the people who
    remember
To say thank You to God for our gifts.

May 1996

Touch of Heaven

What is it like to have a baby
Fall asleep while holding your finger?
It is a soft, precious touch.
It is relaxing, yet exciting.
It is a feeling of trust and importance.
It is so soothing it makes me want to
Fall asleep.
It is a sign of peace and love.
What is it like to have a baby
Fall asleep while holding your finger?
It is a great gift from Heaven.

November 1999

A Handful of Mattie

My fingers stand for
Reader,
Writer,
Black Belt,
Collector,
And friend . . .
My palm stands for
Heartsongs,
Ebullient, spiritual,
Honest, trustworthy,
Brother, uniparental,
Optimistic, inspiring,
Diligent, savant,
Peacemaker, and
"Gift of God" —
My hands raise in prayer for
Giving thanks for my being
Which stands for life.

January 2000

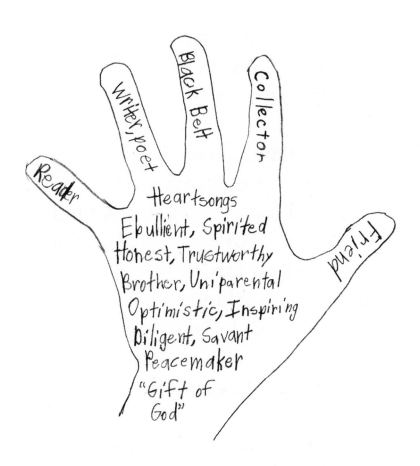

Reader

Writer, poet

Black Belt

Collector

Friend

Heartsongs
Ebullient, Spirited
Honest, Trustworthy
Brother, Uni-parental
Optimistic, Inspiring
Diligent, Savant
Peacemaker
"Gift of
God"

The Language of God

Do you know what
Language God speaks?
God speaks Every-Language.
That's because God made
Everyone and gave
Everyone different languages.
And God understands all of them.
And, do you know what is God's
Favorite language?
God's favorite language is
Not grown-up's language,
But the Language of Children.
That's because children
Are special to God.
Children know how to share,
And they never lose
Their Heartsongs.

April 1996

Making Real Sense of the Senses

Our eyes are for looking at things,
But they are also for crying
When we are very happy or very sad.
Our ears are for listening,
But so are our hearts.
Our noses are for smelling food,
But also the wind and the grass and
If we try very hard, butterflies.
Our hands are for feeling,
but also for hugging and touching so
    gently.
Our mouths and tongues are for tasting,
But also for saying words, like
"I love you," and
"Thank You, God, for all of these
    things."

April 1995

89

Climbing to Heaven

In the winter, trees reach
Up to touch the sky.
Without their leaves,
The trees look like hands
And fingers stretching up
So, so, so high.
And if you look at the
Tallest tree in our backyard,
You can see that it is
So, so, so close to Heaven.
Perhaps we could go out
And climb
Up the tree,
Up the hand,
Up the fingers,
And into the sky.
Then, we could just step
Through the clouds,
And into Heaven.

January 1996

About Angels

Do you know what Angels wear?
They wear
Angel-halos and Angel-wings, and
Angel-dresses and Angel-shirts
   under them, and
Angel-underwear and Angel-shoes
   and Angel-socks, and
On their heads
They wear
Angel-hair —
Except if they don't have any hair.
Some children and grown-ups
Don't have any hair because they
Have to take medicine that makes it
   fall out.
And sometimes,
The medicine makes them all better.
And sometimes,

The medicine doesn't make them all
  better,
And they die.
And they don't have any Angel-hair.
So do you know what God does then?
He gives them an
Angel-wig.
And that's what Angels wear.

January 1995

Believing for the Journey

Every day,
Everyone in the world
Should do at least
One thing nice for others.
Doing so can help each person
Believe in himself or herself
More fully, and
Give confidence that may
Inspire each person
To do more and
More new and good things
For the self,
For others, and
For the world.
Those positive attitudes
And actions
Can be the first of many steps
Towards the journey

For world peace.
And world peace,
Harmony, and
Confidence are essential
For our future.

May 2000

Future Echo

When I swing,
I go everywhere,
And yet,
Nowhere at all.
It's like being
In the middle
Of an echo,
That hasn't left me yet,
And so,
It hasn't come back.
I am between
Yesterday and tomorrow,
But still in my life of now.
When I swing,
I feel so happy,
And excited, and peaceful,
And yet,
I feel a little bit lonely

About the time that
Will come, when I will not be
Able to swing, anymore.
And so, for now,
When I swing,
I move back and forth
In the everywhere
And the nowhere
That is the understanding
Of an echo —
The echo of my spirit
That grows from my life,
And that sounds like
A peaceful, but lonely cry,
For the times
When I swing
Before I die.

August 1999

Vietnam War Memorial

A wall gives structure.
It can divide and block.
It can support and fortify.
It can be a place to display
Photos, writings, awards,
And memories.
But this, is The Wall.
The Wall that gives structure
To the insane losses of a war.
The Wall that represents
A nation divided and blocked.
The Wall that supports too
Many broken hearts and bodies.
The Wall that fortifies the reality
Of dead lives among the living.
The Wall that reflects memories
Of what was, of what is,
Of what might have been,

In photos, in letters and poems,
In medals of honor and dedication,
And in teddy bears, and flowers,
And tears and tears and tears.
This is The Wall,
Born out of pain and anguish
And guilt,
That gives names to the children
Of grieving mothers and fathers
And to the spouses of widows
And to parents of wondering children.
This is The Wall
That echoes sadness and fear,
Yet whispers relief and hope.
This is The Wall.
May we be forever blessed by its
Structure and fortitude and support,
And may we be forever reminded
Of the eternal divisions of war.

February 2000

100

The Tiger Fights a
Dragon in the Purple Sun

When the sun sets,
In the mist,
The tiger and
The dragon fight
In the purple light.
Who wins?
Who knows?
Thy who have
Great Heartsongs know.
The tiger of peace, or
The dragon of anger.

May 1998

Philosophy Glass

Some people see a glass
With some water in it and say,
"Oh yes, that glass is half full!"
Some people see a glass
With some water in it and say,
"Oh no, that glass is half empty!"
I hope that I am one of the
People who is always able to
Look at each of my glasses and
See them as at least half full.
That's very important in life,
Because if you live feeling like
Your glass is half empty, well,
It may as well be empty all the way.

May 1997

On Being a Champion

A champion is a winner,
A hero . . .
Someone who never gives up
Even when the going gets rough.
A champion is a member of
A winning team . . .
Someone who overcomes challenges
Even when it requires creative
    solutions.
A champion is an optimist,
A hopeful spirit . . .
Someone who plays the game,
Even when the game is called life . . .
Especially when the game is called life.
There can be a champion in each of us,
If we live as a winner,
If we live as a member of the team,
If we live with a hopeful spirit,
For life.

September 1999

Peace of Patience

I cannot wait to become
A peacemaker.
I cannot wait to help
The world overcome
Anger, and problems of evil.
I cannot wait for the world
To be peaceful,
And for everyone
To live in harmony.
I cannot wait to grow
And be and overcome.
But, I will wait,
With patience,
And hope, and peace.

November 1999

Faces of Faith

I wish that the people who have
Anger and hatred and sadness
Will remember about their
Heartsongs,
And get them back.
Everyone is born with a Heartsong,
But as we grow up,
Sometimes we forget about it,
Because we don't listen to it enough.
And the people of war, well,
They really need to get them back.
Their Heartsongs really need to live,
Because when we die,
They are what rise up.
I want that to happen to me.
I want my Heartsong to rise up, and
I am trying my best down here on earth.
You really can go to Heaven.

Everyone can.
But sometimes,
You have to sit in ThinkTime
When you lose your Heartsong.
And that is sad because some people
Who go sit in ThinkTime,
They never come back
And some people just think and
    realize,
And then they come back.
But if we remember to listen to our
    Heartsongs,
We will not need to go to ThinkTime.
Our songs will just rise up out of our
    hearts,
And take our spirits straight on to
    Heaven.
I will remember to listen to my
    Heartsong.
I will remind others, especially the
    grown-ups,

To listen to their Heartsongs, too.
And for the people who have forgotten
    theirs,
I will share mine with them.
Maybe they will keep mine, and
Maybe it will remind them of their
    own.
But what really matters is that we
Keep the faces of faith, and
Listen to our Heartsongs, and live
So that we can die and Live again.

July 1996

Welkin

The sky is such
A perfect blue,
It must have
Been painted there.
Even the clouds
Bear witness
To the stroke of
An artist's brush.
This just proves that
God is perfect
At many professions.

February 2000

Pirate-Candy

You know why most people
Don't like black jelly-beans?
Because they're pirate-candy!
Black jelly-beans taste like "pirate."
They smell like pirate.
They're the color of the
Jolly Roger pirate flag.
They're like the little black patch
Pirates wear over their empty-eye.
Black jelly-beans are also the
Pirates' favorite candy flavor,
Because they taste a little bit mean.
But under the hard black-bean
    outside,
Is a soft good-jelly inside
That tastes sweet and nice.
You see,
Most people just taste the dark part.

But I crunch through that nasty bit
And get right to the jelly-bean guts.
So I am the lucky one,
Because I know that most
    pirate-candy
Is actually pretty good stuff.

April 1996

Important Things

When I grow up,
I think maybe
I will be a snowman,
Because when it
Snows outside,
I'll already be cold
And like it.
And children will
Play with me,
And laugh
And sing
And dance
All around me.
And those are important
Things to have happen
When you grow up.

December 1993

Beware, of The Ever-Wolf

I am a werewolf for any moon . . .
When the moon sits full like a
Yellow-white or maybe orange circle
In the dark night sky,
I will grow my fur, and
My long pointy fingernails, and
My longer pointy toenails, and
My two fuzzy tails, and
My icky-sharp'ed fangs, and . . .
I will howl,
Ow, ow, ow, ow-ooooooohhhh!!!!
Under the full moon.
Then, I will come back inside,
And turn back into the
Nice little here-boy that I am . . .
Except that,
I am a werewolf for any moon.
So even if I don't have my fur

And my nails and my teeth
And my lonely, scary howl,
I will be there just the same.
I will be a whenwolf with the sun, and
A whichwolf with the almost moons,
    and
A whywolf with the invisible moon.
But always watch out, and beware,
    because
I am a werewolf for any moon . . .

                                May 1996

At Long Last

Half-empty trees
Scritch at
Ghouly gray skies,
Laughing black crow
Haunts a sound
To the wise,
Orange-toothed
Pumpkins smirk
Jagged tooth grins,
Message is clear:
Halloween now begins!

October 1998

The Left-Over Child

A long time ago, my parents
Had a little girl named Katie.
They thought that they would only
Have this one little child,
But then mommy started growing
Another little baby inside of her.
It was a little boy named Stevie.
But little Katie died, and
Then little Stevie died, and
My parents were alone
Without any children at all.
Then, they grew another baby.
It was a little boy named Jamie.
And then in 1990, they had
Another little boy named Mattie,
And Jamie and Mattie were
Brothers together for a long time.
But then, Jamie died, too,

But Mattie was still alive because
He didn't die like his brothers and
    sister.
Now, he's not really a little brother
    anymore,
But he's not really the only child
    either.
Mattie is the left-over child,
All alone with the parents of dead
    children.

February 1996.

Unanswered Questions

My brother, Jamie died.
His muscles-and-bones
Did not work at all anymore.
His happiness and specialness
Went into Heaven and
His body got buried in
The hole that goes into the ground
And then into the sky and
And then to the Everywhere
And Forever that is Heaven.
I know why he died,
But I also don't know why.
I really don't.
He is happy,
And sometimes I am, too.
And sometimes I am sad
Or angry or scared or confused.
And sometimes I think

That maybe,
I didn't hold his hand tight enough.

December 1993

Anniversary Reflections

I remember the day Jamie died.
Except . . .
I didn't know that Jamie DIED
Because I didn't know
What it was like to look or be dead.
I remember you told me Jamie died,
    and
I remember that his tubing wasn't on
    his trach, and
I remember that you wouldn't let me
Get in bed with Jamie that morning.
But I thought it was because Jamie
    was asleep.
I thought when I got home from
    school that
You would let me get in bed and play
    and read
And be with my brother Jamie.

But when I got home, Jamie was still
  asleep,
Except . . .
He was really dead.
I remember that, but I didn't know that.
I remember all the people coming over
And going into Jamie's room, but
His music was playing, and
His nurses were there, and
He looked just the same in his bed,
So I never really knew he was dead.
I remember the day we went to church
And then to the cemetery to bury
  Jamie's body.
Except . . .
I didn't know that I wouldn't see him
  again.
I remember you put him in that little
  white box,
And you showed me how comfortable
  his body looked,

And I put a picture of us in his hand
With his cross and his Mr. Bear and
　　his Blue-Bunny-Rabbit,
And I knew that we should Never put
　　Jamie in a box on the floor
But it must be okay because
The nurses were helping you.
I remember the little white box in
　　church and
I remember thinking that it was time
　　for Jamie
To knock on the box and we would
　　open it and
He would sit up and yell, "BOO!" and
　　we would all laugh.
I remember that you said this was
A celebration for Jamie at church,
So I knew it was just a game and that
　　he would come out.
Except . . .
He didn't.

And the box got all buried into
    Heaven but under the ground,
With Jamie inside of it, because
He was dead.
I remember the day Jamie died,
And I understand now that it means
    Forever
And that he wasn't asleep and
    couldn't yell "BOO."
But I don't understand why you sent
    me to school that day.
If you knew that dead was Forever,
Why did you send me to school?
I should have stayed home like you,
To be with Jamie before he went
Forever into his little white box,
Because I want to remember Jamie,
Forever.

November 1995

Never-ending Story

Once upon a time,
There was a Jamie and a Mattie.
And for a while,
They were both alive.
But one day,
Jamie died.
And of that,
Mattie cried.
And this story goes
On and on and on
With a Jamie dying
And a Mattie crying,
And on and on like that
Ever- and After-after.

August 1994

Before the Visit

The rising sun sends
Wisps of light through
Streaking clouds,
But the blackbirds play under
The empty willow tree.
The midnight of the fall
Is rising upon us,
And against us.
It is the dawn of winter.
There are things
In the clouds, and
We must be prepared.
We must be watchful,
As the blackbirds,
As the weeping willow,
As the waiting darkness.

December 1997

126

Intensive Sense

In the PICU . . .
I see bright lights,
But there is no sun,
And almost a loss of time.
I hear machines alarming,
But though they ring warnings,
Lives are not always saved.
I feel pain, intense at moments.
But I also feel the hurt of anxiety,
And neither anguish is good for the
    spirit.
Someday,
I will leave the PICU, again.
I will see the sun,
Rising into new days,
But I will know it must set, too soon.
I will hear music sounding,
Ringing from so many instruments,

But most of it will be memories of my
  Heartsongs.
I will feel my spirit rejuvenated,
And I will be filled with hope again.
But, I will feel a sad sense of loss
For the children
Who will be Still
With the anguished sounding loss of
  time . . .
In the PICU.

May 2001

PICU—Pediatric Intensive Care Unit

Rebecca's Reminder

It is sad
When a friend
Dies.
Death becomes
Suddenly
Painful.
Suddenly
Real.
Suddenly
Reminding.
When a friend
Dies,
Perhaps
We should
Suddenly
Remember
How real
Death is,

And wonder
How our
LIFE
Will be,
Suddenly,
Based on
How much of
A friend we are
Now,
Regularly.

November 2000

The Holding-On Family

I'll never let you go, Mommy.
And you never let me go, either.
We'll hold on to each other,
Forever.
We'll never let go.
Even if you get very, very sick,
Or if I get very, very sick,
We'll never let go.
We'll hold on, and
We'll pray for each other,
Together.
Our family already got enough smaller
Without Jamie, and Katie and Stevie.
We need to never let go again.
We'll be a whole family,
Staying together, you and me.
We'll be a holy family,
Praying, together.

We'll be a holding-on family,
Forever.

April 1996

About Wishing

Some people think that
Wishing is childish.
But, wishing is
For everybody.
Wishing can help the
Old feel young, and
Wishing can help the
Young grow into the
Wisdom of age.
Wishing is not
Prayer or magic,
But, somewhere in between.
Like prayer and magic,
Wishing brings optimism,
And wishing brings hope.
And like prayer and magic,
Wishing brings new ideas,
And sometimes,

The touch of new life.
And that, is essential
For our future.

January 2000

Heavenly Greeting

Dear God,
For a long time,
I have wondered about
How You will meet me
When I die and come to
Live with You in Heaven.
I know You reach out
Your hand to welcome
Your people into Your home,
But I never knew if You
Reached out Your right hand,
Or if You
Reached out Your left hand.
But now I don't have to
Wonder about that anymore.
I asked my mommy and
She told me that You
Reach out both of Your hands,

And welcome us with
A great big giant hug.
Wow!
I can't wait for my hug, God.
Thank You,
And Amen.

March 1996

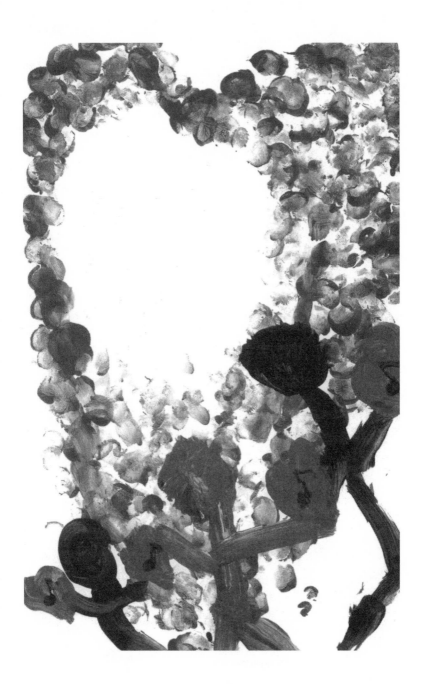

On Growing up (Part V)

We are growing up.
We are many colors of skin.
We are many languages.
We are many ages and sizes.
We are many countries . . .
But we are one earth.
We each have one heart.
We each have one life.
We are growing up, together,
So we must each join our
Hearts and lives together
And live as one family.

September 1996

On Growing Up (Part 1)

I really don't know much
About my toilet.
I need to learn more about it,
And about how it works.
I need to learn all
About my house
Before I grow up,
So I can teach my kids
Before they grow up,
So they can teach their kids
Before they grow up,
And you see, it can just go
On and on and on like that.
There's a lot of learning to do
While we are growing up,
And a lot of teaching
And a lot of learning
While we are all grown up.

January 1996

140

Be a Bird

Birds walk in the sky.
I wonder
What it would be like to
Walk in the sky.
I will be a bird,
And walk in the sky.
The air is
Very, very cold way up high.
And the sun is
Like a bumblebee,
All yellow and round.
And the dark rain clouds are
Like lots and lots of bumblebees,
All angry and buzzing and angry.
The sky is so blue, and
The butterflies are so orange, and
The ground is
So way down below.

October 1993

Sunset

Beautiful things
Are everywhere,
But sunset is so
Soothing and peaceful.
It can send you
Into Dreamland,
Filled with happy thoughts.
And it's all just because
The sunset is God's
Special Tiger's Eye.
A Tiger's Eye is
Sometimes dark and stormy,
Sometimes bright with colors.
A Tiger's Eye is strong
And seeing and knowing,
And it is always a
Symbol of life end energy.
So when you see the sunset,

Through storms and brights,
Think of God,
Our great I AM,
And His beautiful Tiger's Eye.

February 1998

Hidden Treasure

After-the-storm clouds
Are like pirate treasure chests . . .
Dark and gray-black and
Sometimes a little scary looking.
But just look behind as they open . . .
Silver and shiny-gold and
Usually bright and warm, if it's
Still daytime after the storm.

May 1996

Grounded Lesson

Life is a treasure.
People should enjoy it,
Even if digging
To it, or
Through it,
Is a challenge.

February 2000

Tree Song

The trees are singing tonight.
Listen . . . listen and hear . . .
They're singing a song of happiness
    and joy.
They're singing a song of peace and
    thought.
They're singing a song of wonder and
    God.
I do not know the name of the song,
But I know the sound of the music.
I do not know the words of the song,
But I know the feel of the sound.
And the sounds make me feel brave
    and proud.
I feel relaxed and trusting as a lamb.
I am ready to run and play.
I am ready to rest gently.
I am ready to comfort someone.

And, I am ready to follow my
   Shepherd
To a good life, which is Heaven.
The trees are singing tonight.
Listen . . . listen and hear . . .

May 1998

Christmas Stars

In December,
The dark sky of nighttime
Comes very early.
And as soon as the daytime
And then the sunset are all through,
There are lots and lots of
Christmas stars.
We see them everywhere
In the sky with the moon.
It is a present from
Heaven in the sky
To real live people
Who look up.
That is so special.

December 1993

About Watches

I like wearing
Lots of watches
For two reasons.
First,
If they are all set
A little different,
No one's ever
Too late, or
Too early, or
Right on time.
They just "are."
Second,
With all these
Watches on me,
It's like having
"All the time
In the world!"
And never having

To think about
The end of time,
Or about dying.

August 1997

Swinging

So high . . .
Wind tickles my tummy
Plays with my feet
Gives my hair a ride.
So high . . .
Grab a leaf from a tree
Reach a so-far-up branch
See over the edge of my earth.
So high . . .
Meditate on being
Touch all my thoughts
Think about friends
And families and
Brothers and sisters.
So high . . .
Leave this world for a bit
Jump into Heaven for a moment
Then, swing back into my life again.
So high . . .

August 1998

Kindergarten-itis

My stuffed animals and babies
Don't like the big yellow monster.
They don't like that big yellow
    monster
That swallows Mattie up every
    morning,
And then takes him away for so
    many hours
And then brings him back home
And then spits him out "p-tooey"
Right where it ate him in the first
    place.
Even when Mattie tells them,
"It's only a school bus little guys,
I can handle it, don't you worry!"
They still don't like it at all.
But now, there are only
Seventeen days left for that

Big yellow monster to swallow me
And chew me and spit me out
   "p-tooey . . ."
Because summer vacation is
Just around the corner
Where the school bus never comes.

May 1996

Special Things

Isn't it special
How Jamie knows when
I am just a little bit
Too sad?
He is my brother, and
He loves me forever.
And when
I am just a little bit
Too sad,
He sends me
A rainbow to look at,
Or a butterfly to run with,
Or a feather to catch.
And sometimes,
He sends me
All of those things
Even when I am not so sad.
He just wants me to
Be even happier.

August 1994

157

On Being a Good Brother

Some day,
I want to tie Jamie's
Brown moose pants
Onto the end of a balloon,
And send them up to Heaven for him.
Don't you think
That would make him happy?
And it would make all the other
Heaven Angels and Children
     happy, too!
Some day,
We need to do that
Special thing,
Because I want to be a good brother.
I want to do things
That make my Jamie happy.

October 1995

When I Die (Part II)

When I die, I want to be
A child in Heaven.
I want to be
A ten-year-old cherub.
I want to be
A hero in Heaven,
And a peacemaker,
Just like my goal on earth.
I will ask God if I can
Help the people in purgatory.
I will help them think,
About their life,
About their spirits,
About their future.
I will help them
Hear their Heartsongs again,
So they can finally
See the face of God,

So soon.
When I die,
I want to be,
Just like I want to be
Here on earth.

November 1999

I Could . . . If They Would

If they would find a cure when I'm a
  kid . . .
I could ride a bike and sail on
  rollerblades, and
I could go on really long nature hikes.
If they would find a cure when I'm a
  teenager . . .
I could earn my license and drive a
  car, and
I could dance every dance at my
  senior prom.
If they would find a cure when I'm a
  young adult . . .
I could travel around the world and
  teach peace, and
I could marry and have children of my
  own.

If they would find a cure when I'm
grown old . . .
I could visit exotic places and
appreciate culture, and
I could proudly share pictures of my
grandchildren.
If they would find a cure when I'm
alive . . .
I could live each day without pain and
machines, and
I could celebrate the biggest thank you
of life ever.
If they would find a cure when I'm
buried into Heaven,
I could still celebrate with my brothers
and sister there, and
I could still be happy knowing that I
was a part of the effort.

June 2000

Meditation: The Wind in My Heart

This is not a dream.
This is real.
I talk with God, and
Even if my eyes are closed,
I am awake, and I know.
Whichever direction
The wind is blowing,
I follow it.
And when the wind stops,
I stop where it stops,
And I see God.
Sometimes,
God looks like a golden harp
That is shaped like a silver flower.
We talk together about health, and
We talk about how babies
And other people die.
Then I hug and kiss God.

I can do that because
God is every-shape.
Every shape that the world has.
He is a circle, a triangle, every-shape.
He is even invisible.
And, He is even human.
So, we can hug God,
If we know how.
I understand, so I hug Him.
God is everywhere the wind takes me.
The wind takes me to God; and
God takes the wind to me.
It asks me where I want to go
Without even saying anything,
    anyword.
It just knows.
It just knows.
I always see in the wind,
And so, I will follow the wind as it
Moves inside my world and
Inside my house and inside my heart.

I will trust the wind, and
I will let it take me wherever it is
    going,
Because God is in the wind.
God is the wind,
And I am here for God.

August 1996

December Prayer

No matter who you are,
Say a prayer this season.
No matter what your faith,
Say a prayer this season.
No matter how you celebrate,
Say a prayer this season.
There are so many ways
To celebrate faiths,
There are so many faiths
To celebrate life.
No matter who,
No matter what,
No matter how . . .
You pray.
Let's say a prayer
This season,
Together, for peace.

December 1999

On Being Thankful

Dear God,
I was going to thank You tonight
For a beautiful sunrise,
That was pink behind the fog down
  the hill,
And for a wonderful rainbow,
That I ran under pointing to
All my favorite colors,
And for such a great sunset,
That sparkled orange across the
  water.
I was going to thank You tonight
For all of these special gifts,
Except that none of them happened.
But do You know what?
I still love You, God,
And I have lots of other things
That I can thank You for tonight,

Even if You didn't give those
Very special gifts to me today.
It's okay, God,
Because I'll look for them all again,
When my tomorrow comes.
Amen.

November 1995

The Mattie Book

Sometimes,
I wish I could be in a book.
And the book would have
Lots and lots of pages.
When everyone reads it,
They would know
About Jamie, and Katie and Stevie.
They would know
About God and life,
And about love and Heaven
And about playing and feelings
And rainbows and feathers and
Mommies and peacemakers and
Dinosaurs and friends
And all the other important things.
And all of the pages would
Have lots and lots of words,
   filled with

Mattie's thoughts and Heartsongs.
And they would live and teach
Saying "Hooray for Life!" forever,
Even after I am gone.

November 1994

A New Hope

I need a hope . . . a new hope.
A hope that reaches for the stars, and
That does not end in violence or war.
A hope that makes peace on our earth,
    and
That does not create evil in the world.
A hope that finds cures for all diseases,
    and
That does not make people hurt,
In their bodies, in their hearts,
Or most of all, in their spirits.
I need a hope . . . a new hope,
A hope that inspires me to live, and
To make all these things happen,
So that the whole world can have
A new hope, too.

May 1999

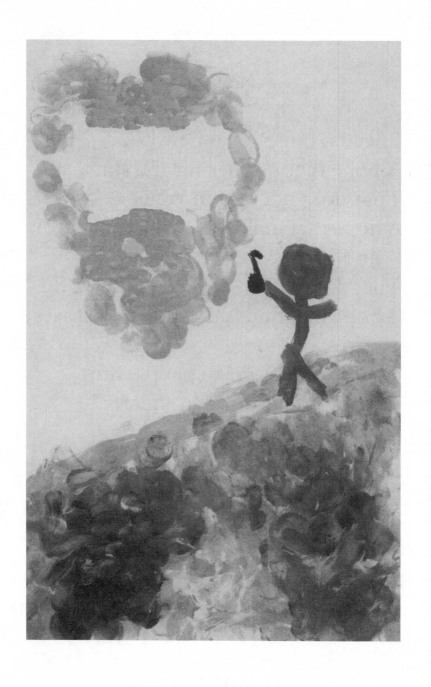

Eternal Echoes

Our life is an echo
Of our spirit today,
Of our essence
As it is,
Caught between
Our yesterday
And our tomorrow.
It is the resounding
Reality of who we are,
As a result of
Where we have been,
And where we will be,
For eternity.

Spring 2000

About the Author (Part II)

Eleven-year-old Matthew Joseph Thaddeus Stepanek, best known as "Mattie," has been writing poetry and short stories since age three. Mattie's poems have been published in a vari-

© Lyn Mox

ety of mediums and he has been an invited speaker for several seminars, conferences and television shows. In 1999, he was awarded the Melinda Lawrence International Book Award for inspirational written works by the Children's Hospice International. He has appeared on *Oprah*, *The Today*

Show, *Good Morning America* and many other programs. In addition to writing, Mattie enjoys reading, collecting rocks and shells, and playing with Legos. He has earned a black belt in martial arts, and in 2001, Mattie served as the Maryland State Goodwill Ambassador for the Muscular Dystrophy Association. In 2002, he will serve as both the National Ambassador and the State Ambassador for the MDA. He lives with his mother, Jeni, in Upper Marlboro, MD, where he is home-schooled.